Superfood Lover's Turmeric Cookbook
Fight Disease and Get Healthy Fast With the Best Turmeric Recipes

DevelopedLife.com

Developed Life Books
4884 W. Hardy Rd
Tucson, AZ 85704
US

Turmeric Cookbook © 2016 C.K. Media Enterprises, L.L.C.. All rights reserved. No part of this book may be used or reproduced in any manner whatsoever, including electronic, digital and Internet usage, without written permission from the author, except for written quotations for critical reviews, or for excerpts used for similar works. The author of this book is not a mental health professional or doctor, and makes no claims to be. The author is not responsible for any consequences that may result from using this information. This book is for entertainment purposes only.

First Printing – 2016

Superfood Lover's Turmeric Cookbook

Table of Contents

Superfood Lover's Turmeric Cookbook 1
Introduction 8
   Get My Books For Free! 8
   A Note About Measurements 10
Getting Started With Turmeric 11
   Curcumin 12
   Turmeric's Vitamins 13
   Cooking With Turmeric 13
Appetizers 15
   Easy Thai Chicken 15
   Tofu Stuffed Cherry Tomatoes 17
   Oven-Fried Potatoes 18
   Spicy Pineapple Fritters 19
   Spicy Orange Hummus 21
   Spicy Bean Spread or Dip 22
   Spiced Mushrooms 23
   Spiced Walnuts 24
   Chicken Coconut Satay Skewers 25
   Chicken Sate With Peanut Sauce 27
   Coconut Bean Slaw 29
   Masala Prawns 31
   Tandoori Mushrooms 33
   Quinoa Pilaf in Lettuce Cups 35
   Minced Prawn Curry Balls 37
   Curried Chicken Wings 38
   Soy Falafel 39

Spinach With Chickpeas 40
Raw Cashew Chickpea Hummus 42
Chicken Lollipops 44
Thai Barbecued Chicken 46
Exotic Falafel 47
Quinoa & Raw Vegetable Salad 48
Curried Eggs 50
Sweet Curry Cucumber Salad Sandwiches 51
Chili Yogurt Mushrooms 52
Cottage Cheese Cutlets 54

Turmeric Entrees 55
Golden Rice 55
Mouth-Watering Fish 57
Couscous With Seven Vegetables 58
Masala Potatoes 60
Chili Chickpea Stir-Fry 61
Turmeric Rice with Eggplant 63
Roasted Cauliflower With Turmeric, Curry & Lemon Pepper 64
Couscous Salad 65
Scrambled Golden Tofu 67
Spicy Potatoes 68
Tofu Pepper Stir-Fry 69
Potato, Tomato and Pea Curry 70
Spicy Chickpea Tagine 71
Lentil Salad 72
Extra Seasoned Chicken Curry 74
Mushroom Masala 76

Turmeric Cookbook

Spinach Pilaf 77

Cauliflower and Green Pea Curry 78

Tuna Curry 79

Butter Chicken 81

Potatoes & Spinach 83

Tandoori Chicken 85

Yogurt Chicken Lettuce Wraps 86

Mashed Eggplants With Eggs 88

A Message from Andrea 90

Introduction

Thank you a lot for buying this book! I hope it will assist with the incorporation of super-foods like turmeric into your lifestyle. After you've done trying out these delicious recipes, please remember that a review on Amazon would really help me to keep going with all this.

Get My Books For Free!

If you bought this on Kindle for a couple of dollars (or on paperback for a few more) I greatly appreciate it. However, keep in mind you also have a chance to receive some of my products for free. This is by signing up to my mailing list. I will periodically run a free promotional tool, and I'll let my subscribers know whenever I do this.

In addition, everybody who signs up receives a FREE copy of my book: The 20 Most Deceptive Health Foods

The point of this book is to educate readers about what foods are actually healthy, and which ones are not.

It's a must-have to take with you to the grocery aisles.

You can join the exclusive mailing list right now at the following link:

http://www.developedlife.com/andreasilver.

This is my completely free gift for my subscribers.

A Note About Measurements

I generally create these recipes using all or part of the metric system. This is more handy for exact measurements. There are many sites like metric-conversions.org where you can do conversions if you're not sure how to use metric or if you don't have a scale. If you are from the UK or USA and you are confused at all, go to this exact address: http://www.metric-conversions.org/volume/milliliters-to-us-cups.htm (this is for ml to US cups, as an example simply switch to UK cups or a different measurement that fits your country).

Through using ml this way for any type of recipe, you get exact amounts versus approximations.

Getting Started With Turmeric

The main courses and appetizers presented in this cookbook are among the most flavorful I've ever created. Many of these recipes are a fusion of Western cooking, and East-Indian cuisine. You'll find Southeast Asian influence, as well. I guarantee these are some of the tastiest recipes you'll ever try.

So, let's talk a little about the thematic ingredient of this recipe collection: turmeric. It's one of the four great super-foods I'm exploring in this series, and certainly one of the tastiest.

In essence, turmeric is a kind-of root-vegetable, otherwise known as a rhizome (a continuously growing, underground stemmed-plant) which has a leafy green above-ground appearance. It's related most closely to ginger, and turmeric root actually looks like quite similar.

When the root is boiled, dried, and then crushed—it creates a rich orange-yellow powder. The flavors of the root are also enhanced by doing this, creating that spicy and earthy flavor which is almost hard to compare to any other flavor but turmeric itself.

Since time immemorial, East and Southeast-Asian countries (India, Pakistan, Bangladesh, Thailand, and many other countries) have taken advantage of the many awesome properties of the plant. One of the most common uses is not actually as a food, but as a dye. Turmeric remains as a common textile dye, and a natural food coloring. The golden yellow color of turmeric is the origin of the color of yellow curries throughout the world.

Extraordinarily, I still meet people in the USA whom have never even tasted turmeric before, despite its long history in other parts of the world (I am always flabbergasted by how unwilling many people are to go outside of their comfort zones, travel to new places, or eat exotic foods).

Curcumin

The benefits of turmeric are largely related to the substance isolated from the powder, which is also the source of the strong dying properties, and that is curcumin.

For millennia, turmeric has been a natural cure for many different conditions. It's impossible to know how natural remedies first came about; however, it's possible that from a very early point, people recognized how curcumin consumption led to longer lifespans and less disease, and so it became an all-purpose medicinal solution.

The curative effects of curcumin, and why turmeric is often considered a "super-food", relates to its proven anti-inflammatory effects. These are produced by the antioxidant curcuminoids.

Recent medical research has shown how inflammation is related to a vast amount of diseases, including heart-disease, many types of cancers, and diabetes to name just a few illnesses. Many dietitians therefore believe that reducing inflammation can prevent serious diseases. This can be accomplished by eating healthier, exercising, avoiding simple carbohydrates (white sugars and white breads) and other sources of sugar, and supplementing your diet with natural ingredients like turmeric.

Another reason to incorporate an anti-inflammatory into your diet is to prevent or reduce the effects of various arthritic conditions, such as rheumatoid arthritis and osteoarthritis.

Turmeric's Vitamins

In addition to the anti-inflammatory effects, turmeric consumption can also fortify your diet with the following vitamins and minerals:

- Ascorbic acid
- Beta Carotene
- Calcium
- Flavonoids
- Iron
- Niacin
- Potassium
- Vitamin E
- Zinc

It's no wonder turmeric is a super-food!

Cooking With Turmeric

It's best to buy turmeric in a bulk supply. You can order a bag of turmeric on Amazon. After it arrives, store it in a dry, cool place. Keep it sealed, and keep it away from too much light exposure.

It's been observed that the health effects of turmeric / curcumin seem to be reduced if it's excessively cooked. Therefore, it's safe to assume the healthiest recipes in this book are those that are raw. And if the recipe allows for it, try to add the turmeric seasoning at the end—after the rest of the dish has been cooked. If this cannot be done, however, the turmeric is still healthy—don't worry.

Other experts suggest to stabilize it with acid. Curcumin tends to disintegrate if it's pH becomes too alkaline. When turmeric is included with lemony salad recipes, for instance, one could say you're eating it at the healthiest state possible.

Getting Started With Turmeric

Now that you understand a little about turmeric, you're probably eager to start cooking with it. The great thing about this super-food is that it opens up a whole new range of culinary possibilities. If you've ever had curry and loved it, I have good news—that's just the tip of the iceberg. These recipes will allow you to explore turmeric in many other flavorful ways—ranging from various different cultures.

Enjoy!

Appetizers

Easy Thai Chicken

Servings: About 6

Ingredients:

- 290 g can Thai-Choice satay sauce
- 400 ml Thai-Choice coconut milk, canned
- 4.92 ml turmeric powder
- 750 g chicken strips

Directions:

- Best prepared with grilling bamboo.

- Soak the bamboo skewers in water approximately two hrs.

- After two hours, take the bamboo skewers out from the water and stab the meat strips on them. Combine 350 ml of the coconut milk with turmeric powder & marinate for a

Appetizers

minimum period of an hour, if you want more flavor then you need to marinate it for longer.

- Grill the satay's & during grilling use the leftover turmeric & coconut milk mixture to baste. Serve with the heated satay sauce.

Tofu Stuffed Cherry Tomatoes

A great turmeric-rich *vegan* snack.

Servings: About 4

Ingredients:

- 226.79 g crumbled tofu
- 1.23 ml garlic powder
- 2.46 ml oregano
- 226.79 g tomatoes, cherry
- 1.23 ml turmeric
- Pepper and salt

Directions:

- Remove the stems from the cherry tomatoes & make a cut in the top of each tomato carefully; a small hole would work fine.

- Remove & save the tomato pulp.

- Mix tofu, spices & tomato pulp together in a small bowl.

- Stuff the tofu mixture into the cherry tomatoes & serve chilled.

Appetizers

Oven-Fried Potatoes

Servings: About 8

Ingredients:

- 1.23 ml turmeric
- 2.46 ml cumin
- 1.23 ml cayenne
- 907.18 g russet potatoes
- Pepper & salt
- Olive oil cooking spray

Directions:

- Preheat your oven to 400 F / 200 C.

- Spray oil over the oven racks.

- Wash the potatoes using cold water and slice them crosswise into thin rounds.

- Transfer the sliced potatoes to a baking pan and spray well with oil.

- Add the seasonings and toss well to coat. Arrange the sliced potatoes on the oven racks, in a single layer and put the racks in the middle of the oven.

- Bake the potatoes approximately half an hour, until a deep, golden-brown crust forms and become tender. Serve hot.

Spicy Pineapple Fritters

Hot and sweet mixed together. Habanero has a great flavor, but don't underestimate how much heat it packs!

Servings: About 6

Ingredients:

- 473.18 ml pineapple, fresh & chopped
- 2 eggs
- 236.59 ml flour
- 1 sliced scallion
- 14.79 ml chives, fresh & diced
- 1 minced habanero
- 2.46 ml turmeric
- 118.29 ml milk
- 3 minced sage leaves
- Olive oil, for frying
- Pepper and salt

Directions:

- In a high speed blender, blend together the eggs, scallion, chives, habanero, sage leaves, turmeric, milk, flour, pepper and salt until well mixed and smooth.

- Put the mixture in a bowl, preferably large & add the pineapple chunks. Stir well to evenly coat.

- Heat oil in a heavy pan. When the oil would be heated through, drop the batter by spoonfuls & fry for few minutes, until browned. Remove the fritters & drain on the paper towels.

Appetizers

- Season with salt & garnish with chives.

- You may either serve it hot or at room temperature, or even cold. It doesn't matter. Booyah.

Spicy Orange Hummus

This recipe is a little bit unusual, I'll admit. I first had it at a restaurant in Los Angeles, then eventually dug up a recipe online, which I later modified a bit and started experimenting with it. It's an original combination of flavors, to say the least. And really good.

Servings: About 8

Ingredients:

- 425.24 g chickpeas, canned & drained
- 1 garlic clove
- 29.58 ml onions, chopped
- 4.92 ml soy sauce, low sodium
- 59.14 ml orange juice
- 29.58 ml tahini
- 59.14 ml parsley leaves, fresh
- 29.58 ml rice vinegar
- 4.92 ml Dijon mustard
- 1.23 ml each ground ginger, ground coriander, ground turmeric, ground cumin, paprika & salt

Directions:

- With the food processor on, drop the garlic, onion, and parsley through the food chute, and process for few minutes, until minced.

- Now put the orange juice & the leftover ingredients & process until smooth and mixed well.

- Serve with crudite or pita triangles.

Appetizers

Spicy Bean Spread or Dip

A bit of turmeric can spice up (and healthify…I made that word up) your dip.

Servings: About 2

Ingredients:

- 425.24 g beans, canned and of your choice
- 4.92 ml chili salsa, mild
- 1.23 ml garlic powder
- 0.25 ml turmeric

Directions:

- With about ½ liquid from the can, using a food processor, fork or masher, mash the beans.

- Mix together the spices.

- Serve with toasted pita bread or lightly steamed or raw vegetables.

Spiced Mushrooms

Fresh spices brings this vegan mushroom dish to life.

Servings: About 4

Ingredients:

- 4.92 ml cumin, ground
- 500 g button mushrooms, whole
- 4.92 ml turmeric, ground
- 4.92 ml cardamom, ground
- 4.92 ml coriander, ground
- 4.92 ml nutmeg, ground
- 4.92 ml black pepper, ground
- 78.07 ml olive oil

Directions:

- In a large glass, ceramic or plastic bowl, place the mushrooms.

- In a jug, preferably small, mix together the cardamom, 2/3 of oil, cumin, nutmeg, pepper, turmeric & coriander.

- Put this mixture over the mushrooms & to coat the mushrooms, toss well in the mixture.

- Set aside and let it marinate approximately 15 minutes.

- Over high heat settings, heat a wok until hot. If you don't own a wok, well just settle for a frying pan.

- Add leftover oil & mushrooms. Stir-fry until golden & just tender, approximately five minutes.

- Serve hot.

Appetizers

Spiced Walnuts

Servings: About 3

Ingredients:

- 709.77 ml walnuts
- 2.46 ml turmeric
- 0.25 ml cayenne
- 29.58 ml chili powder
- 2.46 ml cumin
- 59.14 ml olive oil
- 2.46 ml salt

Directions:

- In a large skillet, mix together the olive oil, chili powder, cumin, turmeric & cayenne.

- Over low heat settings, heat the oil; until very hot (but don't allow the oil to smoke).

- Take the skillet away from the heat and add the walnuts to the oil & stir well until evenly coated.

- Spread the walnuts in a shallow baking pan, preferably towel-lined & bake at 150C/300F until crisp, approximately 10 minutes.

- Sprinkle salt and let it cool at room temperature. Pack the prepared walnuts in fancy jars. Sell for obscene amounts of money at your local farmer's market.

Chicken Coconut Satay Skewers

Servings: About 12

Ingredients:

- 680.38 g chicken breasts, skinless & boneless
- 40 wooden skewers
- 29.58 ml lemon juice
- 6 peeled clove garlic
- 78.07 ml coconut milk
- 2.46 ml whole cumin seed, ground
- 6 shallots
- 4.92 ml coriander leaves, ground
- 14.79 ml brown sugar
- 1.23 ml turmeric
- 2.46 ml salt

Directions:

- Before the grilling process, soak the skewers in water, preferably cold approximately two hours.

- Cut the meat into pieces, preferably about 2 cm.

- In a bowl, preferably medium sized, arrange the pieces.

- Whirl together the coconut milk, garlic, shallots, sugar, lemon juice, coriander, cumin, salt & turmeric either in a blender or food processor and form a smooth paste.

- Combine meat with the mixture & let it marinate in the fridge approximately two hours, covered.

- Thread onto the skewers without crowding, approximately four pieces per skewer.

Appetizers

- Broil or grill approximately five minutes, until browned and crisp, but still juicy, turning occasionally to cook evenly.

Chicken Sate With Peanut Sauce

Sate, or satay, are dishes of grilled or skewered meat popular across the eastern parts of the world. Sambal oelek is a type of chili paste that you can find at any ethnic grocer.

Servings: About 4

Ingredients:

Sate Marinade
- 14.79 ml ginger, fresh & minced
- 680.38 g chicken breast tenders
- 14.79 ml sambal oelek
- 118.29 ml shallot, chopped (approximately 4)
- 4 garlic cloves
- 4.92 ml fish sauce
- 9.85 ml coriander seeds
- 14.79 ml soy sauce, low sodium
- 2 whole cloves
- 29.58 ml sugar, dark brown
- 0.25 ml nutmeg, freshly ground
- 2.46 ml black peppercorns
- 9.85 ml olive oil
- 2.46 ml turmeric

Peanut Sauce
- 118.29 ml creamy peanut butter, reduced-fat
- 44.37 ml lime juice
- 4.92 ml hot chili sauce
- 14.79 ml soy sauce, low sodium
- 4.92 ml hot paprika, dark brown
- 9.85 ml sugar, dark brown
- 78.07 ml water

Directions:

Appetizers

- Preheat the broiler.

- To make the sate; place the sate ingredients (except the chicken breast) in a food processor & process for few minutes, until smooth. Place the mixture & chicken in a large plastic bag, preferably zip-top. Seal & let it marinate in refrigerator approximately 10 minutes.
- To make peanut sauce, in a medium bowl, mix together the sauce ingredients and whisk, stirring well.

- Remove the chicken from the bag & discard the extra marinade. Thread the chicken on eight wooden skewers, preferably 12". Place the skewers on the rack of a roasting pan or broiler evenly coated with cooking spray. Broil until done, approximately 10 to 12 minutes. If needed, turn the chicken once or twice.

- Serve the chicken sate with peanut sauce.

Coconut Bean Slaw

Servings: About 6

Ingredients:

- 946.0 ml salted water
- 118.29 ml chopped bell pepper
- 236.59 ml navy beans or black-eyed peas
- 2.46 ml turmeric
- 236.59 ml coconut milk
- 118.29 ml chopped onion
- 2.46 ml cayenne pepper
- 59.16 ml olive oil
- 1 large tomato
- 59.14 ml parsley
- 1 head lettuce
- 4.92 ml salt

Directions:

- Put salted water in a large skillet and cook the beans until tender, approximately an hour, drain & keep them aside.

- Over medium high settings in a medium sized sauce pan, heat the oil; add onion, bell pepper, salt and cayenne; sauté approximately two to three minutes, until onion is tender; add beans & continue cooking for two min more; stir in the coconut milk; cook until sauce sticks to the beans.

- Refrigerate the mixture until it's very cold, and to let the spices to meld with the beans. Leave it in the refrigerator for a day.

- On a platter, preferably large, arrange the individual lettuce leaves and place half cup serving of coconut/bean mixture on

Appetizers

each lettuce leaf & top the leafs with parsley & tomatoes; serve as an appetizer or salad.

Masala Prawns

Servings: About 8

Ingredients:

- 73.94 ml tomato ketchup
- 1 onion, chopped
- 946.36 ml shrimp, shelled & cleaned
- 2.46 ml turmeric powder
- 9.85 ml coriander powder
- 2.46 ml cinnamon
- 9.85 ml cumin powder
- 4.92 ml chili powder
- 1 bunch cilantro
- 14.78 ml olive oil
- salt

Directions:

- Mix the prawns with turmeric & salt, mixing well. Keep them aside approximately half an hour.

- Over medium high heat settings in a frying pan, heat the oil.

- Add onions & fry till oil begins to leave and onions starts to become brown.

- Now, add the prawns & stir fry for few minutes until it becomes hard.

- Add the powdered spices & mix well.

- Add the ketchup, when the prawns are just about done.

Appetizers

- Mix with three tbsp. of water & let the prawns cook approximately 5 to 7 minutes, on medium high heat settings.

- Garnish with fresh cilantro, and serve hot.

Tandoori Mushrooms

Servings: About 4

Ingredients:

- 340.19 g cremini mushrooms, trimmed & wiped clean
- 4.92 ml salt or to taste
- 2 roughly chopped garlic cloves, peeled
- 44.37 ml Greek yogurt, plain
- 4.92 ml cumin, ground
- 59.14 ml lemon juice, fresh
- 4.92 ml hot paprika or 4.92 ml red chili powder
- 2.46 ml turmeric, ground
- 14.79 ml roughly chopped gingerroot, fresh & peeled (approximately 4cm piece)
- 177.44 ml sour cream
- 2.46 ml white pepper
- 29.58 ml vegetable oil

Directions:

- Combine cumin, garlic, chili powder, ginger, salt, white pepper and turmeric in a food processor; pulse until everything is chopped finely, scraping down the sides occasionally.

- Add in 1 tbsp. of vegetable oil, and the lemon juice, puree; add the yogurt and sour cream and pulse just for a moment to combine.

- Transfer the marinade to either a bowl or a plastic bag that's re-sealable. Add the mushrooms; cover & refrigerate for a minimum period of half an hour.

Appetizers

- Heat a tandoor to 250 C/500 F. You can also use a broiler on a "high" setting.

- Thread the mushrooms onto skewers & cook in the tandoor approximately 2 to 3 minutes, until lightly browned. Baste with 1 tbsp. of oil & continue cooking approximately a minute or two more until browned & tender (3 to 4 minutes per side on the broiler or grill, basting with the oil).

Quinoa Pilaf in Lettuce Cups

Healthy and as vegan as it gets, if that's your thing.

Servings: About 4

Ingredients:

- 236.59 ml quinoa, picked & rinsed well
- 1.23 ml garam masala
- 2.46 ml turmeric
- 1 head boston lettuce, leaves separated
- 1.23 ml ginger, ground
- 14.79 ml pine nuts
- 29.58 ml chopped dried cherries
- 1 grapefruit, zested, plus 2 tablespoons juice
- 354.88 ml water
- 1 red onion, medium & finely chopped
- 1.23 ml coriander, ground
- 29.58 ml olive oil
- Kosher salt & black pepper, freshly ground

Directions:

- To remove the outer coating, rinse the quinoa well in a sieve (mesh strainer) & then over medium high heat settings, toast in an iron skillet for few minutes, until the toasty quinoa aroma begins.

- Over medium heat settings in a small saucepan, bring the one and a half cups of water & quinoa to a boil. Decrease the heat settings & simmer approximately half an hour, until curly white germ shows and quinoa is cooked, covered.

- In the meantime, over medium heat settings in large skillet, warm the olive oil. Add the onion & spices after the oil

Appetizers

shimmers, and sauté until the spices are very fragrant & the onion has softened.

- Stir in the fruit & pine nuts & sauté approximately a minute or two.

- Ensure that the water has been absorbed completely and then add the cooked quinoa to the skillet. Stir in the grapefruit juice & grapefruit zest. Taste & season with pepper & salt, to taste. To ensure that the flavors seep into the quinoa, remove it from the heat and let sit approximately 10 minutes.

- Serve in lettuce cups.

Minced Prawn Curry Balls

Servings: About 4

Ingredients:

- 1 egg
- 453.59 g prawns, shelled & dried
- 1 onion, large & roughly chopped
- 14.79 ml ginger, fresh & grated
- 1 green chili
- 2 garlic cloves
- 2.46 ml black pepper, ground
- 14.79 ml parsley, chopped
- 2.46 ml turmeric
- 113.39 g olive oil
- Breadcrumbs
- 2.46 ml salt

Directions:

- Put the prawns, turmeric, chili, garlic ginger, onion, salt & pepper in a food processor and give them a quick blitz. Make sure the ingredients are finely chopped and mixed.

- Put the egg in the mixture & mix well.

- Create golf-ball size balls from the mixture. Coat with breadcrumbs and refrigerate approximately half an hour.

- In a pan, add the olive oil & fry the prawn balls for a few minutes, until golden. Drain on kitchen paper. Garnish with the chopped parsley. Serve warm.

Curried Chicken Wings

Any fan of spicy chicken wings will love this "east meets west" style recipe.

Servings: About 8

Ingredients:

- 32 chicken wings
- 14.79 ml turmeric, ground
- 9.85 ml hot curry powder
- 14.79 ml cumin, ground
- 9.85 ml chili powder
- 14.79 ml lime rind, grated
- 2 clove garlic, crushed
- 14.79 ml coriander, ground
- 177.44 ml vegetable oil
- 14.79 ml hot paprika

Directions:

- In the thickest part of each wing, make two deep cuts.

- In a bowl, preferably large, mix together the remaining ingredients.

- Add the chicken wings & mix well.

- Refrigerate for a minimum period of three hours or for overnight.

- Cook the wings in a heated oiled barbecue, until tender & browned on both sides, uncovered.

Soy Falafel

Servings: About 12

Ingredients:

- 236.59 ml breadcrumbs
- 3 cake tofu, pressed & mashed (approximately 1020.58 g)
- 236.59 ml onion, finely chopped
- 118.29 ml sesame seeds, toasted
- 22.18 ml dark sesame oil
- 44.37 ml tamari soy sauce
- 59.16 ml tahini
- 3 minced garlic cloves
- 14.79 ml turmeric
- 59.14 ml parsley, fresh & chopped
- 1.23 to 2.46 ml cayenne
- 59.16 ml lemon juice, fresh
- 14.79 ml cumin, ground
- 44.37 ml vegetable oil
- Black pepper, to taste

Directions:

- Make the tofu more absorbent & firmer by pressing it. To press, keep the tofu stuck between three flat plates. Make sure that the sides of the tofu shouldn't crack but become bulged. Let sit approximately half an hour & then pour out the water.

- Mix together all of the ingredients in a large bowl.

- Form into balls, preferably 2 cm each & bake at 350 F/175 C on a greased baking sheet approximately half an hour, until a little crusty on the outside & golden, but moist on the inside.

Appetizers

Spinach With Chickpeas

Servings: About 6

Ingredients:

- 2602.49 ml baby spinach, rinsed & shaken dry
- 1 medium onion, finely chopped
- 793.78 g chick-peas, canned & drained
- 1 clove garlic, cut in half
- 0.59 ml turmeric
- 2.46 ml cumin
- 0.59 ml cayenne pepper
- 2 pimientos, drained & sliced
- 29.58 ml olive oil
- Pepper and salt

Directions:

- Over medium-high heat settings in a large, lidded skillet, heat the oil.

- Put the garlic in the skillet & cook until golden, approximately a minute or two; using a slotted spoon, remove & discard.

- Add the cumin & onion, cayenne and turmeric to the skillet and cook until soft, approximately 5 minutes, stirring frequently.

- Add the chickpeas & stir until evenly coated with the spices & oil.

- Stir in the spinach with a small quantity of water. Cover; cook until wilted, approximately for 5 minutes.

- Uncover & stir in the pimientos & continue cooking for a few more minutes, until the liquid evaporates, stirring gently.

- Season to taste & serve.

Appetizers

Raw Cashew Chickpea Hummus

This vegan recipe requires sprouted chickpeas. This can be a fun process, and is a great dish for all of you raw-food fanatics out there.

Servings: About 6

Ingredients:

- 118.29 ml raw cashews
- 591.47 ml sprouted chickpeas
- 2 garlic cloves
- Juice of 1 lime
- 1.23 to 2.46 ml cayenne
- 1 grated ginger root, preferably into 2cm slices
- 4.92 ml ground coriander
- 2.46 ml ground pepper
- 29.58 ml mint
- 4.92 ml ground cumin
- 0.25 ml cinnamon
- 29.58 ml cilantro
- 4.92 ml sea salt
- 0.25 ml turmeric
- 59.14 ml olive oil, extra virgin

Directions:

- To make the chickpeas sprout, rinse & soak 1 cup of dried chickpeas for a day, adding fresh water half way through. Rinse & place in a clean glass jar. After they have soaked, using elastic, place the cheesecloth over the top. You will need to rinse the chickpeas twice or thrice a day and they will take approximately 1 to 4 days to sprout. The moment the "tail" reaches approximately 1 cm long, you can eat the chickpea sprouts.

- Grind the garlic and cashews in a pestle or food processor until crushed to small bits.

- Add in the sprouted chickpeas, ginger, herbs/spices & salt. Grind for few minutes, until the chickpeas are small bits.

- Add in the olive oil & lime juice & blend until smooth. To get the desired consistency, you may have to add a splash of water as well.

- Enjoy!

Appetizers

Chicken Lollipops

Small chicken-wing variant snacks.

Servings: About 8

Ingredients:

- 24 chicken wings, separated at upper wing joint.
- Peanuts, crushed & roasted

For Marinade:
- 29.58 ml cilantro, fresh & chopped
- 283.49 g coconut milk, canned
- 9.85 ml garlic, minced
- 29.58 ml brown sugar
- 9.85 ml ginger, minced
- 2.46 ml chili pepper, dry
- 59.14 ml soy sauce
- Juice of 2 limes
- 9.85 ml turmeric
- 4.92 ml curry powder

Directions:

- Remove the skin from the chicken wings.

- Form a lollipop shape by scraping the flesh from one end of bone to the top knuckle and then arrange them in a shallow dish.

- Transfer marinade over the chicken. Cover & refrigerate for overnight.

- Put the marinade aside, and barbeque the chicken until golden and crispy, approximately 6 to 8 minutes per side.

- To make the dipping sauce, bring the rest of the marinade to a hard boil for approximately a minute. Top the lollipops with crushed & roasted peanuts.

Appetizers

Thai Barbecued Chicken

Servings: About 4

Ingredients:

- 8 chicken thighs

For Marinade Paste
- 44.37 ml Asian fish sauce
- 44.37 ml garlic, minced
- 2.46 ml black pepper
- 29.58 ml cilantro, fresh & chopped
- 14.79 ml sugar
- 4.92 ml curry powder
- 4.92 ml turmeric, ground

Directions:

- In a food processor, place all of the marinade ingredients & process until you get a paste.

- Put the chicken thighs in a plastic bag, preferably sealable, with the marinade.

- Coat the chicken well by turning the bag a few times. Refrigerate for overnight and to distribute the marinade, turn the bag occasionally while it soaks.
S
- Lift the chicken thighs from the marinade & put them over low coals on a grill, lightly greased.

- Cook approximately 45 minutes, until the meat close to the bone is no longer pink, turning frequently.

Exotic Falafel

Servings: About 12

Ingredients:

- 2 beaten eggs
- 118.29 ml scallion, finely minced
- 946.36 ml chickpeas, well cooked
- 44.37 ml tahini
- 2.46 ml cumin, ground
- 3 garlic cloves, crushed
- 2.46 ml turmeric
- 44.37 ml fine breadcrumbs or 44.37 ml flour
- 118.29 ml celery, finely minced
- 1.23 ml cayenne
- flour (for coating)
- 0.25 ml black pepper
- 7.39 ml salt

Directions:

- Mash the chickpeas well using a potato masher and then mix it with other ingredients. Chill this mixture.

- Make the batter into balls, preferably 2cm (about 1") in diameter with floured hands.

- Dust each ball lightly with the flour.

- In a heavy skillet, heat a 2-inch pool of oil to 365 F/185 C.

- Fry the falafel for few minutes, until golden & serve warm.

Appetizers

Quinoa & Raw Vegetable Salad

Servings: About 4

Ingredients:

- 709.77 ml chicken or vegetable stock
- 236.59 ml rinsed quinoa
- 4.92 ml turmeric
- 118.29 ml celery, finely diced
- 44.37 ml Italian parsley, flat leaf
- 177.44 ml onion, sweet
- 118.29 ml carrot
- 59.14 ml olive oil, extra virgin
- 177.44 ml fresh beet, washed & peeled
- 118.29 ml radish
- 4.92 ml fresh garlic, diced & extra fine
- 118.29 ml bell pepper
- 4.92 ml Dijon mustard
- 59.14 ml balsamic vinegar or red wine
- Pepper and salt

Directions:

- Dice all the vegetables finely.

- Toast the rinsed grain with onion and then add the stock with turmeric, until the liquid is absorbed, approximately 15 minutes.

- Now prepare the dressing by combining the vinegar, oil, mustard, garlic, parsley, pepper & salt.

- Toss well with vegetables and quinoa

- If possible, let it sit overnight or for a minimal period of two hours.

Curried Eggs

Servings: About 24

Ingredients:

- 24 eggs
- 2 green onions, minced
- 59.14 ml celery, minced
- 14.79 ml curry powder
- 236.59 ml mayonnaise, light
- 0.59 ml each pepper & salt
- 2.46 ml turmeric
- 0.59 ml cayenne

Directions:

- In a large pot, place the eggs & cover them with water. Let the eggs boil. Turn off the heat when eggs begin to boil & let them sit in the pot approximately 10 minutes.

- Peel the eggs, and then cut them lengthwise & remove the yolks. You need to now add the yolks to the other ingredients & mix all of it together in a bowl.

- Dab the yolk mixture in the whites & enjoy.

Sweet Curry Cucumber Salad Sandwiches

I'll tell you right now—these are addicting.

Servings: About 12

Ingredients:

- 177.44 ml mayonnaise (I prefer all-natural olive-oil mayo)
- 2 seedless English cucumbers, preferably long
- 7.39 ml lemon juice
- 4.92 ml curry powder
- 14.79 ml honey
- 1.23 ml turmeric
- Melted cheese (try gouda)
- sliced bread

Directions:

- Chop the cucumber. You can make thin slices of cucumber or cubed chunks. Try both.
- Wisk together the lemon juice, mayonnaise, curry powder, turmeric and honey in a separate bowl. Adjust the seasonings as per your taste, if required, you may add a larger quantity of curry powder or honey. Add in the cucumber & stir well for few minutes, until combined well.
- Spread the melted cheese on the sliced bread and spoon the curried cucumber filling on & top with another slice of bread.

Appetizers

Chili Yogurt Mushrooms

A vegan dish that's a bit Mediterranean, a bit Western.

Servings: About 4

Ingredients:

- 453.59 g thickly sliced cremini mushroom
- 2 onions, large & chopped
- 118.29 ml plain yogurt
- 4 garlic cloves, large & crushed
- 396.89 g tomatoes, canned & chopped
- 2.46 ml chili powder
- 4.92 ml garam masala
- 2.46 ml sugar
- 4.92 ml turmeric, ground
- Cilantro, fresh & chopped
- 59.16 ml olive oil
- Salt, to taste

Directions:

- Over medium-high heat settings in a large wok or skillet, heat the oil. Add the onion & sauté, until they are golden, approximately 5 to 8 minutes, stirring frequently.

- Stir in the garlic & sauté for two minutes more.

- Add the tomatoes & their juice & mix well. Stir in the garam masala, turmeric & chili powder. Continue cooking approximately three more minutes.

- Add the mushrooms, salt, and sugar, to taste and cook until soft and tender & they have given off their liquid, approximately 8 to 10 minutes.

- Turn off the heat & stir in the yogurt, a small quantity at a time, stirring well. Taste and if needed, adjust the seasoning according to your taste.

- Sprinkle fresh cilantro & serve.

Appetizers

Cottage Cheese Cutlets

Servings: About 4

Ingredients:

- 473.18 ml cottage grated cheese
- 0.25 ml turmeric powder
- 236.59 ml onion, chopped
- 3 to 5 green chilies, fresh, washed & finely chopped
- 2.46 ml ginger-garlic paste
- 9.85 ml gram flour
- Salt & Red chili powder, to taste
- Olive oil

Directions:

- Mix together the cheese in a large bowl and then add the ginger-garlic paste, green chilies, gram flour, turmeric powder, salt, red chili powder to taste & lastly the onions.

- Form round balls from the mixture, approximately 1" or about 2cm in diameter.

- Flatten each ball gently.

- In a frying pan, preferably flat, heat the oil and place the flattened balls.

- Shallow fry the balls on either side for few minutes until golden brown.

- Drain the balls on clean paper towels.

- Serve hot with coriander & mint chutney or tomato ketchup.

Turmeric Entrees

Golden Rice

Let's get started with a basic, easy-to-make turmeric dish. This could be a great side-dish, or a meal in itself. You can create large batches of this to eat all week.

Servings: About 4

Ingredients:

- 473.18 ml broth, preferably chicken, or vegetable broth if you're going vegan.
- 236.59 ml rice, long-grain
- 118.29 ml onion, chopped
- 2.46 ml turmeric, ground
- 9.85 ml Italian seasoning
- 14.79 ml olive oil
- 236.59 ml peas, frozen
- Salt to taste

Turmeric Entrees

Directions:

- Over medium heat settings in a large skillet, heat the oil. Add onion & cook until softened, approximately 3 minutes, stirring frequently. Add turmeric, rice and Italian seasoning; cook approximately 2 more minutes, stirring frequently.

- Stir in the chicken broth and allow it to boil. Decrease the heat settings to low. Cover & simmer approximately 15 minutes. Stir in the peas and cover again. Cook until rice is tender, approximately 5 to 8 minutes.

Mouth-Watering Fish

Here's a dish if you want a nice bit of protein to go with your golden rice.

Servings: About 2

Ingredients:

- 59.16 ml natural yogurt
- 400 g (about two) trout filets, fresher the better
- 1 finely minced hot red chili pepper
- 9.85 ml lemon juice
- 4.92 ml garlic, crushed
- 9.85 ml ginger, fresh & grated
- 2.46 ml turmeric powder
- 4.92 ml each cumin & coriander powder
- Coriander, fresh (to garnish)
- 4.92 ml salt

Directions:

- In a large bowl, preferably non-reactive, mix all the ingredients together (don't add the fish), mix well. Coat the fish pieces evenly & keep them aside approximately half an hour.

- Spray cooking spray on a pan, or use olive oil, and heat over medium heat settings. Put the fish filets on the pan. Cook approximately 3 minutes, flip over & cook until cooked through, approximately a minute or two (time depends on the thickness of your chosen filets).

- Sprinkle a little coriander over the filets and serve warm.

Couscous With Seven Vegetables

This is a very middle-eastern inspired dish. The cinnamon and couscous is an especially popular combination in such countries. The addition of paprika, turmeric and cumin creates some of the most flavorful veggies you'll ever eat.

Servings: About 6

Ingredients:

- 473.18 ml couscous
- 591.47 ml stock, vegetable or chicken
- 118.29 ml peas, fresh
- 1.23 ml cinnamon
- 118.29 ml red onion, chopped
- 2.46 ml turmeric
- 118.29 ml red pepper, diced
- 2.46 ml ground cumin
- 118.29 ml zucchini, diced
- 59.14 ml carrot, diced
- 118.29 ml turnip, diced
- 1.23 ml paprika
- 44.37 ml coriander, fresh & chopped
- 1.23 ml black pepper, ground
- Salt, to taste

Directions:

- In a pot over medium heat settings, heat the chicken or vegetable stock. Add turmeric, black pepper, paprika, cinnamon & cumin. Simmer approximately two mins.

- Add red pepper, carrots, onion, turnips, zucchini & peas. Simmer until vegetables are softened, approximately 5 to 7 mins. Increase the heat settings to high & let it boil. Now, stir the couscous in the mixture. Cover; remove from the heat and let it stand approximately 5 minutes. Uncover & using a fork, fluff. Season with salt & sprinkle coriander over it.

Turmeric Entrees

Masala Potatoes

This is a highly nutritious Indian recipe.

Servings: About 6

Ingredients:

- 8 roughly chopped Desiree potatoes, skin left on
- 4.92 ml turmeric
- 9.85 ml garam masala
- 4.92 ml chili, dried & chopped
- 14.79 ml cumin, ground
- 4.92 ml black mustard seeds
- 500 ml water
- 4.92 ml kalounji seeds (can omit, but is more traditional)
- 14.79 ml coriander, ground
- 4.92 ml pepper & salt

Directions:

- Grind all the spice-ingredients and mix well.

- Dry-fry the spices until sweet-smelling then add the potatoes, raw & diced with water. Cover; cook until potato is just cooked, approximately 20 mins (checking after every few minutes).

Chili Chickpea Stir-Fry

Another great, diverse mixture of healthy spices, and healthy chickpeas.

Servings: About 4

Ingredients:

- 411.06 g can tomatoes, diced, no-salt-added & un-drained
- 2 can chickpeas, rinsed & drained (approximately 878.83 g)
- 118.29 ml chopped carrot
- 177.44 ml chopped celery
- 9.85 ml paprika
- 236.59 ml chopped onion,
- 9.85 ml cumin, ground
- 2 minced garlic cloves
- 1.23 ml red pepper, ground
- 2.46 ml turmeric, ground
- 1.23 ml cinnamon, ground
- 4.92 ml ginger, ground
- 29.58 ml cilantro, fresh & chopped
- 14.79 ml fresh lemon juice
- 29.58 ml tomato paste, no-added-salt
- 354.88 ml water
- 1.23 ml each black pepper, ground & salt
- 9.85 ml olive oil

Directions:

- Over medium high heat settings in a saucepan, preferably large, heat the oil. Add celery, onion, garlic, & carrot to the pan; cook approximately 5 minutes, stirring constantly.

Turmeric Entrees

- Stir in the turmeric, cumin, ginger, paprika, cinnamon, black pepper, salt & red pepper; cook approximately a minute, stirring constantly.

- Add tomato paste, water, tomatoes and chickpeas and let it boil for some time. Decrease the heat settings & cover. Simmer approximately 20 minutes & stir in the cilantro & juice.

Turmeric Rice with Eggplant

Servings: About 4

Ingredients:

354.88 ml broth, preferably chicken
1 large eggplant
1 garlic clove, minced
1 onion, chopped
14.79 ml turmeric
1 bay leaf
236.59 ml basmati rice
0.06 ml thyme
29.58 ml coconut oil
Pepper and salt

Directions:

- Slice the eggplant into circular slices or cubes. Sauté with some coconut oil for 2-3 minutes on each side.
- Melt some more of the coconut oil, add garlic and onion to the pan. Cook approximately a minute or two, until softened.
- Add turmeric and rice; stir to coat.
- Add the leftover ingredients & bring to boil. Cover: simmer approximately 17 minutes.
- Stir in leftover olive oil, remove the bay leaf & serve.

Roasted Cauliflower With Turmeric, Curry & Lemon Pepper

An excellent, vegan-friendly dish that's plentifully healthy.

Servings: About 4

Ingredients:

- 4.92 ml lemon pepper
- 9.85 ml curry powder
- 1 head cauliflower
- 9.85 ml turmeric, ground
- 4.92 ml salt
- 59.14 ml olive oil

Directions:

- Preheat your oven to 450 F / 225 C. Line a baking sheet, preferably large with foil, preferably heavy duty.

- Cut the cauliflower into steaks, preferably ¾" and then into bite-size pieces.
- Mix spices, salt & oil in a large bag, preferably a zip-lock.
- Add the cauliflower pieces & coat them gently by tumbling.
- Spread out the pieces on a baking sheet & roast until desired degree of doneness, approximately 20 minutes.

Couscous Salad

Lots of vegetables and plenty of flavor. Vegan-friendly.

Servings: About 4

Ingredients:

- 1 red bell pepper, diced
- 2 unpeeled garlic cloves
- 1 yellow bell pepper, diced
- 1 eggplant, small & diced
- 255.14 g couscous, cooked
- 1 diced zucchini
- 4.92 ml cumin seed
- Paprika or chili powder
- Turmeric (a healthy amount)
- Freshly ground black pepper
- Olive oil, extra virgin
- Salt, to taste

Directions:

- Boil about 300 ml of salted water in a saucepan, preferably medium sized.

- Add the oil & turmeric and then the couscous.

- Take the saucepan away from the heat. Cover & allow standing approximately 5 mins.

- Put the couscous onto a platter, preferably flat & separate the grains using a fork.

Turmeric Entrees

- In a frying pan, heat 4 tbsp. of oil & then add the cumin seeds and garlic.

- Put the diced vegetables in the frying pan & sauté approximately 10 minutes, seasoning with pepper & salt.

- In a large bowl, mix together the vegetables & couscous; stir well.

- Sprinkle with paprika or chili powder.

Scrambled Golden Tofu

Another great recipe for the meat-conscious.

Servings: About 2

Ingredients:

- 14.79 ml nutritional yeast
- 453.59 g firm tofu
- 2.46 ml onion powder
- 29.58 ml soy sauce, low sodium
- 2.46 ml turmeric
- Pepper, to taste

Directions:

- In a large bowl, crumble the tofu. Add the remaining ingredients & stir well until evenly coated.

- Heat in a skillet, preferably oiled until the mixture starts becoming slightly brown, approximately 8 to 10 minutes.

- Serve as a hearty breakfast or side-dish.

Turmeric Entrees

Spicy Potatoes

A great flavorful entrée or side-dish.

Servings: About 4

Ingredients:

- 2.46 ml red chili powder
- 44.37 ml cilantro leaves, freshly chopped
- 2.46 ml fennel seed
- 14.79 to 29.58 ml vegetable oil
- 2.46 ml turmeric
- 907.18 g peeled potatoes
- 2.46 ml cumin seed
- Coarse salt

Directions:

- Slice the potatoes into rounds, and then dice these sliced potatoes further into small cubes, preferably evenly-sized.

- Take the minimum quantity of needed oil, and using a non-stick pan or wok & over high heat settings, fry these cubed potatoes. Decrease the heat settings & cover. Add chili powder, turmeric and a small quantity of salt, followed by the leftover spices, when the potatoes are half done. Combine the mixture & stir. Put the lid again on the pan.

- Make sure that the potatoes don't get too soft and when they are nearly ready, take the lid off, increase the heat settings & stir-fry and let any excess liquid evaporated. Garnish with cilantro, fresh and serve warm.

Tofu Pepper Stir-Fry

A great vegan turmeric option that's full of spice and flavor.

Servings: About 6

Ingredients:

- 29.58 ml green pimientos, dried or 14.79 ml green chilies, canned
- 453.59 g firm tofu
- 14.79 ml Italian seasoning
- 2 green onions, chopped or 14.79 ml onion powder
- 1.23 ml turmeric
- 14.79 ml soy sauce
- 1 green bell pepper, chopped
- 1 to 2 tomatoes, ripe & chopped
- 2.46 ml salt
- black salt

Directions:

- Using your hands, crumble the tofu.

- Mix tofu & everything else together in a large skillet (don't add the tomatoes) and heat approximately 8 to 10 mins.

- Put the tomatoes in the mixture & continue heating approximately 5 to 8 more minutes, until thoroughly heated.

Turmeric Entrees

Potato, Tomato and Pea Curry

A classic healthy curry dish.

Servings: About 3

Ingredients:

- 473.18 ml potatoes, peeled & cubed
- 1 onion, large & finely sliced
- 1 to 2 mild chilis, green
- 4.92 ml cumin, ground
- 2.46 ml turmeric, ground
- 1 tomatoes, large & chopped
- 9.85 ml coriander, ground
- 4.92 ml gingerroot, fresh & grated
- 2.46 ml black pepper, ground
- 9.85 ml garlic, chopped
- 236.59 ml peas
- 236.59 ml hot water
- 4.92 ml salt
- 14.79 ml cooking oil

Directions:

- In a large saucepan, heat the oil & fry onion until golden & soft. Stir in turmeric, garlic, chili, ginger, salt and pepper. Continue cooking approximately 2 to 3 mins and then add the potatoes; stir well.

- Add hot water and the leftover ingredients. Continue to simmer until all the vegetables are cooked through.

- Serve this curry with rice & side dishes.

Spicy Chickpea Tagine

Tagine, or Tajine, is a Moroccan dish traditionally served in an earthen-pot. For our purposes, we can skip the pot—unless you happen to just have one lying around.

Servings: About 2

Ingredients:

- 1.23 ml turmeric
- 425.24 g chickpeas, freshly cooked or canned
- 1.23 ml cumin
- 1 chopped onion
- 1.23 ml cayenne pepper or harissa
- 425.24 g can tomatoes, diced
- 1.23 ml ginger
- 14.79 ml cilantro, fresh & finely chopped
- 1.23 ml each salt & black pepper, or to taste
- 14.79 ml Italian parsley, fresh & finely chopped
- 1.23 ml cinnamon
- 29.58 ml olive oil

Directions:

- Put oil into a shallow casserole (or tagine) & cook onions for a few minutes, until golden & soft.

- Now add all of the remaining ingredients & stir well. Cover; cook approximately half an hour, over low heat settings.

- Serve hot with bread, preferably a Middle Eastern pita of some type.

Lentil Salad

A really good side-dish or meal in itself! Note the precise blend of spices which packs a ton of flavor.

Servings: About 4

Ingredients:

- 118.29 ml currants, dried or 118.29 ml raisins or 118.29 ml cranberries, dried
- 29.58 ml apple cider vinegar
- 7.39 ml stone ground mustard
- 226.79 g lentils, dry
- 7.39 ml maple syrup
- 0.59 ml nutmeg, ground
- 4.92 ml pepper
- 0.59 ml cinnamon, ground
- 1.23 ml cardamom, ground
- 0.59 ml cayenne pepper
- 2.46 ml cumin, ground
- 0.59 ml cloves, ground
- 1.23 ml coriander, ground
- 1 red onion, finely diced
- 1.23 ml turmeric
- 44.37 ml capers, drained
- 4.92 ml salt
- 44.37 ml olive oil

Directions:

- Rinse the lentils well using cold water, drain in a colander. Place the lentils in a pot & cover with water. Bring the mixture a boil and then decrease the heat settings & allow it to simmer approximately 15 minutes. After every 5 minutes, don't forget to check the lentils for desired doneness. Once the lentils are cooked through, drain them & rinse under cold water & place them aside.

- Make the dressing in a small bowl by whisking together the vinegar, olive, maple syrup, spices & mustard.

- Gently combine the dressing and lentils in a large serving bowl. Add the cranberries, capers and onions & stir well to combine. Just before serving, you can add some optional ingredients such as greens, cheese, or herbs,

Extra Seasoned Chicken Curry

Here's a 'secret' recipe that is extra flavorful.

Servings: About 6

Ingredients:

- 236.59 ml coconut milk
- 14.79 ml coriander, ground
- 1360.77 g chicken pieces
- 2.46 ml turmeric, ground
- 22.18 ml chili powder
- 4.92 ml mustard seeds
- 7.39 ml cumin seeds
- 4.92 ml fenugreek seeds
- 1 onion, large & sliced
- 3 leaf curry, fresh
- 44.37 ml vegetable oil
- 9.85 ml ginger paste
- 4.92 ml garlic paste
- 29.58 ml fresh lime juice
- 9.85 ml black pepper
- 473.18 ml water
- 7.39 ml salt

Directions:

- In a bowl, preferably large, arrange the chicken pieces & season them with coriander powder, turmeric powder, black pepper, salt, and chili powder. Cover the bowl with a lid & let it refrigerate for an hour.

- Over medium heat settings in a large pan, heat the oil. Fry the fenugreek, mustard seeds, cumin seeds, curry leaves, and onion in oil approximately five minutes. Stir in the ginger pastes and garlic & cook for two more minutes. Add water and chicken pieces & cover with lid, stirring frequently. Cook for another half an hour.

- Stir in the coconut milk & cook until almost dry, stirring frequently. Stir in the lime juice & cook until dry.

Mushroom Masala

A delicious and *vegan* option for masala.

Servings: About 4

Ingredients:

- 236.59 ml tomato puree
- 1 cinnamon stick
- 14.79 ml minced garlic
- 236.59 ml finely chopped red onion
- 4.92 ml coriander, ground
- 29.58 ml vegetable oil
- 4.92 ml chili powder
- 226.79 g sliced mushroom
- 1.23 ml turmeric
- Cilantro
- 2 cloves

Directions:

- Over medium high heat settings in a large pan, heat the oil & first add the cloves followed by the cinnamon stick. Fry both the ingredients for half a minute and then add the onions & sauté for few minutes more.

- Add the coriander, chili powder, turmeric and garlic along with a small quantity of water & sauté until the onions soften. Add the mushrooms, tomato puree and salt & simmer on low heat approximately 5 to mins. Garnish with cilantro. Serve hot with rice!

Spinach Pilaf

Servings: About 4

Ingredients:

- 2 tomatoes, seeded & diced
- 4.92 ml cardamom, ground
- 2 bag spinach leaves, which is approximately 566.99 g or 3 bunches, washed & stems trimmed
- 4.92 ml coriander, ground
- 1 onion, large & diced
- 14.79 ml cumin, ground
- 473.18 ml cooked basmati rice
- 4.92 ml turmeric, ground
- 59.16 ml olive oil
- 9.85 ml salt

Directions:

- Heat 2 tbsp. of olive oil over medium-high heat settings in a large skillet. Sauté spinach with salt until spinach leaves are wilted. Remove the spinach & drain off any liquid.

- Wipe out the skillet & put the remaining olive oil over medium-high heat settings. Sauté onion approximately 2 to 5 minutes until lightly browned.

- Decrease the heat settings to medium-low & add cardamom, cumin, turmeric and coriander. Stir to combine the ingredients well.

- Add reserved spinach, tomatoes and cooked rice and cook, just until the rice is warmed through, stirring gently to mix the ingredients.

Cauliflower and Green Pea Curry

Another delicious vegan curry option.

Servings: About 6

Ingredients:

- 473.18 ml green peas
- 9.85 ml mustard seeds
- 3 minced garlic cloves
- 2.46 ml turmeric, ground
- 1 onion, large & finely chopped
- 59.14 ml water
- 1 head cauliflower, cut into florets, preferably bite-sized
- 9.85 ml ginger, fresh & minced
- 59.14 ml coconut oil
- 2.46 ml red pepper flakes
- 118.29 ml parsley, fresh for garnish
- Black pepper, fresh ground to taste
- 4.92 ml sea salt

Directions:

- Over medium heat settings in a large skillet, melt the coconut oil. Add turmeric & mustard seeds and sauté approximately half a minute, until they start to pop. Add onion & sauté approximately 7 minutes, until translucent. Add the ginger and garlic, and sauté until fragrant.

- Add cauliflower & sauté approximately 5 minutes, until lightly browned. Add the peas, water, red pepper, salt & pepper. Cover and decrease the heat settings to medium low. Cook, until tender, but not mushy, stirring occasionally. Garnish with parsley & serve in a platter or bowl.

Tuna Curry

Servings: About 4

Ingredients:

- 236.59 ml coconut milk
- 453.59 g tuna, in cubes, preferably 2"
- 9.85 ml tamarind paste, to taste
- 14.79 ml vegetable oil or coconut oil
- 2 green chilies, long, sliced in ½ & seeded
- 3 chopped clove garlic
- 9.85 ml ginger, chopped
- 2 sliced tomatoes
- 4.92 ml black mustard seeds
- 2 thinly sliced shallots
- 236.59 ml water
- 4.92 ml turmeric
- Sea salt

Directions:

- Mix 1 cup water & turmeric together in a saucepan, preferably medium sized. Add tuna & season it with salt. Place the tuna over medium-low heat settings and let it simmer.

- Cook approximately two minutes, turning once. Remove the tuna cubes from the heat. Over medium heat in a sauté pan, preferably large, add the oil. Add the mustard seeds, ginger and garlic the moment it starts simmer, & cook for two more minutes.

Turmeric Entrees

- Add chilies, shallots & tomatoes and cook for a minute. Add approximately 1/3 cup cooking water, tuna, tamarind, coconut milk & salt to taste, stir well. Cover & let it simmer, approximately 8 to 10 minutes, until the sauce has slightly thickened & blended.

Butter Chicken

This is a classic Indian recipe that's become famous around the world, yet not everyone knows the secrets to prepare it.

Servings: About 4

Ingredients:

- 2 chicken breasts, large & boneless
- 4.92 ml ginger
- 14.79 ml tomato paste
- 1 crushed garlic clove
- 4.92 ml chili powder
- 177.44 ml cream, fresh
- 4.92 ml turmeric
- 1 chopped onion
- 4.92 ml cinnamon
- 2.46 ml garam masala
- 28.34 g olive oil
- 4.92 ml salt

Directions:

- Sauté garlic & onion in olive oil.

- Slice the chicken breasts into pieces, preferably bite-sized.

- Combine salt with the spices; toss the chicken pieces until coated well.

- Sauté each side of the chicken until golden brown.

- Stir in the tomato paste & cream.

Turmeric Entrees

- Cover the pan and let it simmer until cooked through, approximately 10 minutes.

- Sprinkle with Garam Masala.

Potatoes & Spinach

A healthy dose of greens in this vegan Indian-style side-dish.

Servings: About 2

Ingredients:

- 200 g waxy potatoes, peeled & cubed
- 2 chopped garlic cloves
- 300 g spinach, fresh
- 59.16 ml coconut oil or 59.16 ml olive oil
- 1 to 2 green chili, chopped with seeds
- 2.46 ml cumin, ground
- 4.92 ml garam masala
- 2 chopped onions
- 2.46 ml coriander, ground
- Ginger, fresh & roughly chopped, preferably 1"
- 4.92 ml cumin seed
- 14.79 ml cream, fresh
- 4.92 ml turmeric
- Salt

Directions:

- Cook the spinach with ginger, garlic, green chilies & the onions approximately 5 to 10 minutes in a pan.

- Remove from pan & blend to get a fine puree & set aside.

- Meanwhile boil the potatoes with turmeric and salt approximately 10 minutes, until done and then set aside.

Turmeric Entrees

- Over medium high settings in a pan, heat the coconut oil & fry spinach-onion paste along with the cumin seeds & simmer for some time.

- Add the cumin powder, cooked potatoes, garam masala & coriander and a small quantity of water, if required.

- Simmer till the flavor is absorbed by the potatoes, for a few minutes. If desired, add fresh cream.

Tandoori Chicken

One of the tastiest and most popular Indian chicken recipes.

Servings: About 8

Ingredients:

- 226.79 g carton plain yogurt
- 0.25 ml turmeric
- 680.38 g chicken breasts, boneless & skinless (cut into strips)
- 4.92 ml cumin, ground
- 7.39 ml ginger, fresh & grated
- 9.85 ml paprika
- 0.25 ml cayenne pepper
- 2.46 ml coriander, ground
- 19.71 ml lemon juice, fresh
- 1 minced clove garlic
- chutney

Directions:

- Arrange the chicken pieces in a plastic bag, preferably large.
- Mix the remaining ingredients together and transfer the mixture in with the chicken and then seal the bag.
- Let it marinate for a minimum period of 6 hours or for a complete day in a refrigerator.
- Preheat the broiler.
- Drain the chicken pieces and place them on the broiler rack & broil approximately 12 to 15 minutes until done, turning halfway through.
- Serve the chicken with chutney and an appetizer (side-dish).

Turmeric Entrees

Yogurt Chicken Lettuce Wraps

A tasty lunch or snack.

Servings: About 2

Ingredients:

- 2 chicken breasts, cut into small pieces, preferably bite-sized
- 1 firm lettuce head
- 2.46 ml garam masala
- 1 shallot, small, cut into thin slivers, or use 1 white onion.
- 2.46 ml turmeric
- 2 to 3 minced garlic cloves
- 29.58 ml chili sauce
- 236.59 ml yogurt, plain
- 59.14 ml scallion, chopped
- 2.46 ml cumin
- 29.58 ml cream
- 2.46 ml chili powder
- 0.75 ml pepper
- 2.46 ml salt

Directions:

- In a bowl, preferably large sized, mix all the ingredients together except the lettuce. Let it marinate approximately an hour or two in a refrigerator.

- Over medium high heat settings in a large skillet, heat a dash of olive oil.

- Pour the chicken/yogurt mixture into the pan & cook approximately 10 minutes, until sauce has slightly evaporated and thickened and the chicken is cooked through. Add the cream & continue cooking for a minute or two.

- Spoon approximately three tbsp. of mixture into each lettuce leaf & wrap. If needed, secure it with toothpicks.

Mashed Eggplants With Eggs

This is a Mediterranean dish of Turkish or Lebanese origin. It makes for a hearty, small meal.

Servings: About 4

Ingredients:

- 1 eggplant
- 3 beaten eggs
- 1 tomatoes
- 2 garlic cloves
- 1 onion, cubed
- 4.92 ml tomato paste
- 1.23 ml cinnamon
- 0.29 ml steak sauce
- 4 flat bread
- 1.23 ml chili powder
- 2.46 ml turmeric
- 14.79 ml olive oil

Directions:

- Preheat your oven to 375 F /190C and roast the garlic & eggplant.

- Add tomato during the last 10 minutes of roasting.

- Add oil in a large pan and add the ingredients in the following order: onion, spices, tomato paste & veggies from the oven (peeled & mash them)

- Cook this down and add a few drops of steak sauce (A1). This creates a slightly tangy and robust secret flavor.

- Move to side cook eggs half way stir into eggplant & serve with bread, heated.

A Message from Andrea

Thank you so much for taking the time to read this book. I hope that this was of some benefit to you.

You can find many more books like this one I've created by checking out my Amazon page at the following address: http://www.amazon.com/Andrea-Silver/e/B00W820AR6/.

You can also get in touch with me personally at AndreaSilverWellness@gmail.com if you have any questions or ideas.

Printed in Great Britain
by Amazon